EITHER, ORPHEUS

EITHER,

ORPHEUS

DAN DISNEY

UWA PUBLISHING

First published in 2016 by
UWA Publishing
Crawley, Western Australia 6009
www.uwap.uwa.edu.au

UWAP is an imprint of UWA Publishing
a division of The University of Western Australia

THE UNIVERSITY OF WESTERN AUSTRALIA

National Library of Australia
Cataloguing-in-Publication entry:
Disney, Dan, author.
either, Orpheus / Dan Disney.
ISBN: 978 1 742588 19 3 (paperback)
Australian poetry—21st century.
A821.4

Cover design by Design by Committee
Typeset in Cochin by Lasertype
Printed by Lightning Source

This project has been assisted by the Australian Government through
the Australia Council for the Arts, its arts funding and advisory body.

Australian Government | **Australia Council for the Arts**

Acknowledgements are due to editors of the following publications, where excerpts from or versions of some of these texts first appear: *Arc* (Canada), *Australian Book Review*, *Australian Poetry Journal*, *Axon*, *Best Australian Poems*, *Cordite Poetry Review*, *foam:e*, *Inknagir* (Armenia), *Island*, *Meanjin*, *New Writing* (UK), *Of Nepalese Clay* (Nepal), *Orbis Litterarum* (Denmark), *Poetry Salzburg Review* (Austria), *Plumwood Mountain*, *Postcolonial Text* (Canada), *Southerly*, *Southword* (Ireland), and *The Warwick Review* (UK).

A few hundred kilometres from the Château de Muzot, this book began in the shade of Bisalta, a twin-peaked northern Italian mountain where locals talk of a peasant farmer tricking the devil in a pact for his soul. The second section was developed in Zeytun, on the outskirts of Yerevan. The rest of the poems were either snatched in Seoul or found wandering the drumlins of Annaghmakerrig, in Ireland.

Sincere thanks to the Literature Board of the Australia Council for their generous financial support of this project. Also to the Australian Centre at the University of Melbourne for conferring the Vincent Buckley Poetry Prize, which enabled a reading (and writing) tour of Ireland. Poems from *either, Orpheus* received the Gwen Harwood Poetry Prize, and have been shortlisted for the Blake Prize and the Max Harris Prize.

Special thanks to the Quaglias and Maccarios, Mkrtich Tonoyan and the Aghamalyan family, Evelyn Conlon, Marie Cullen and Paul Ó Colmáin, Claire Chambers, Steffen Hantke, Jordie Albiston, Kevin Brophy, Leonie Starnawski and, especially, Sun-Ha Lee.

little things (a prelude)

N a grey city filled with office buildings that scraped the underfloor of the clouds, in a grey city of factories run by well-greased machines that never slept in too late (and after all, who could sleep with the to-and-fro, all the shuffling hours of the day), in that city of shuddering systems at work, no-one noticed it at first. It made page five of a two-bit weekly when it was found on a deceased estate. It was put in a box. It left. A second-rate detective was employed to find it. It was found on the tallest steeple in town. It was locked away. It escaped. As the sun rose, three dailies wore the headlines on their fronts. Mouths fell open; shadows buzzed and rushed while lounge rooms flickered, lit with reports of it. The mayor, archbishop, three doyen clamoured to make their welcomes. As the sun rose the next day, all strode a lighter stride. Talkshow hosts raved. Breakfasts hummed. Politicians warbled and screenplays were writ. Nothing in their spiny libraries told them a thing of anything like it. What need for the gods now? It was wooed by portraitists in shining dentures, and offered the keys then leadership of the city which (a little less grey) was alive with it. The city began to forget; brass domes soon popped from the central square, each dawn a blast and trill of self-worship. Scholars headached wisps of their theories. Machines were less well-greased, sleep sounder, workers in their places slower. The city began to forget. The city began to forget and then (yes) the city forgot, then forgot it had forgotten and then, at that moment and quick as it had come, it left. Cemeteries sat blank and sunken-eyed, waiting beyond the hills while the city clicked, whirred, and remembered. Fists shook from out the drear; human nature abhors a vacuum, after all. Suburbs nodded in brick veneer and, in the days to come, the shuffling had never seemed so loud. The sky hurled its weather, nothing else. Nights once more electric. The only thing that had changed (each assured the other) was that everywhere everyone was certainly correct, and that nothing at all had changed.

part one

But how human!

Kierkegaard, Either/Or

How the sound of a bird-cry moves us —
any strong voice first formed long ago!

Rilke, Sonnets to Orpheus

I spent the first years of my life in a valley

        sitting in woods muttering the occult business of little folktales;

              madness sometimes works

amid the machines, kept running elegiacally by large sets of hands

        sweeping populations of crow from each momentary wholeness

              I spent the first years of my life in a valley

enchanted by the noise of complex human emotion: it was

        big trouble in tweed jackets, the very wide landscapes of modern man

              and this is why madness sometimes works

(a tradition with its own lost imps/holograms)

        in a wilderness of anthropological models, inside the encyclopedias of kids

              I spent the first years of my life in a valley

conscious as animals inside hotelroom dreams, with

        TV screens jamming on runaway wars crackling away; maybe this

              is why madness sometimes works

a flash of ancient feeling telepathed from unseen, watching minds

        (there's an indefinite number of possibilities if

              you concentrate like a good bird), so: you spend the first years of

                      your life in a valley

        where madness sometimes works

                          (Ted Hughes)

'what we think has everything to do with what we're looking at'
the Helens and Michaels drifting groundwork like claymation, on-duty and everyday
inside moods and blue jeans, outliers of the infinite

carrying huge attics behind their eyes, walls covered with impressionism
while arrangements of bird conglomerate like unattainable dénouement in landscape
'what we look at has everything to do with what we're thinking'

chimes a brotherhood of Stephens, roaming colonially
while handing animal pelts to professors hissing like dustjacket photographs
in gravity, stars fixing a tone where outlines of the infinite

bathe men concentrating like x-ray, exclaiming whenever *is*-ness slams
underneath their hats, Felicities motioning in the too-audible verbs of mild applause,
'how we think has everything to do with what we're looking at'

they'll venture, radiating in a whelm of semi-silent bloodlines, side-by-side
and the dead calling cautionary fugues from underneath hills, upward
skulls through loam, outliers of the infinite

squeezing together in the elemental dim across dining room carriages, passing
through an afternoon in the outer circumferences of Monday, where a Charles intones
'what I look at has everything to do with what
I think' (textures of this world make outlines of the infinite ...)

(Charles Wright)

as *all children know, truth*   is a snake eating its own tail
while householders whinny ethics across dining rooms of thought
and this might be the last thing that can be said

for any generalissimo inside a behaviour army
critical-eyed amid the jaunty peasant societies (noon markets, storytelling, pigs, perhaps a bench)
and as *all children know, truth*   is self-polishing, a bust of bronze

shining a slew of reality across ancestral paths
where the dead pick turnips, shake-boned to narratives arriving by cartload
and this might be the last thing that can be said

dogs barking brio up their roads
to the next command centre, where gentlemen from the avant-garde critique cartoons
and as *all children say, truth*   is the future's loudest part

where cats and physics momentarily *freeeze!* (a place
afternoons can dull to whispered manifestos) and where pre-existence
might be the last thing that can be known

eyes bulging from inside cliché, where
shadow hurls grappling devices amid impedimenta buried by weather
and where, as *all children know, truth*   is a snake eating its own tail
this might be the last thing that can be said

(Paul Muldoon)

I argue about this with my analyst

two forces cancelling one another out, avoiding the wonder

of wrecked endings, sometimes it takes

so long for afternoons to pass (dressed just slightly off)

doormen polite as avalanches, asking me to wait: I argue

bliss is improbable (life cannot be one's continuing

orgasm) so surprise is promoted to the front rank

... you can sample people, look at the nice wine, I have

many arguments with my analyst but on the whole it's chatty

and at the end we say 'you're happy?' then we say

'The End', and sometimes the afternoons go past, resolved

as blurred photographs and all that

blank space up front: arguing about this with my analyst

it takes so long for afternoons to pass

(John Ashbery)

without history, strange instrument with meaning in it, my notes are glossaries
      from an outpost, propagandistic exile tracts
            in a language of ruined ground, bones murmuring

and my voice habit-fashioned, Byzantine with slow
      fables in abstract weather, cosmopolitan and floundering
            without history, strange instrument of meaning

the panoramas bucolic, expressing absolutes overplayed with light
      ashore to fault-lined archaeologies
            of language, where ruined grounds of bone murmur behind lore

genocidally transferred to sunny forgetfulness and I
      am nailing crops of bookcase to horizons, empty
            without history (strange instrument with meaning in it), repeating

the austere phrasings of New World discovery – check one two *∂uh ∂uh ∂uh* – home
      no longer an 'elsewhere but   ' *here*, language in bones
      murmuring, 'we ask

that you please
      edit all behaviour inside these carnal woods', because
            without history's strange instrument, our sound is loanwords
            divesting ground (ruined now) of its bone language

                                        (George Seferis)

tension accumulates in the optic nerve: eyes snap open

and bluish figures jerk past windows, velvety spirits from unknown shores

but otherwise, no change

  folk operate their blinds and the dawn

vulcanises vague intuition, the silken air is torn like skin,

    a brooding material essence smears heavily

        over things

while remnants of a night-seeing crowd grasp the moment: dust-covered and

wonder-struck (crawling and hopping, erotic, refined) rolling in gutters, spasmodic with reason

  nipping the optic nerve, eyes snap open and

penetrate a pre-morning of wire bristle; sponge; rough iron;

animal or peach down, pelt of horse or dog; morbid plastic, human; art, pissoir, bird and otherwise

no change

  folk operate their blinds and the dawn

vulcanises vague intuition, and the silken air is torn like skin,

    a brooding material essence smears heavily

        over things

while processions begin to raise long hats, clicking stories off their tongues

arms dangling in the nude above shining puddles, parklands of old hearts half-smiling

  while tension accumulates in the optic nerves: eyes snap open to arcades of brutal coffee, elbows, breathing

fecund and virile – mouths open-doored, municipal benches awaiting patterns in pale haze

but no change here: folk open their blinds

and dawn vulcanises vague intuition, the silken air tears like skin,

and a brooding material essence smears heavily

over things

as fingertips flex, slow beasts at hypotheses crossing acreage

where forgotten shapes pace messed cages under chimney stacks: here, tension

accumulates in each optic nerve, eyes snap open

but otherwise, no change

folk operate their blinds and the dawn

vulcanises vague intuition; the silken air is torn like skin,

a brooding material essence smears heavily

over things

Nausea (Jean-Paul Sartre)
vs 'Tactilism' (Filippo Tommaso Marinetti)

in neat little red brick towns, voices

       cross the scurf of lawn, neighbours straining bent at fences

faces screaming, smiles contort

       church bells toll for those who'd praise, schoolteachers

hum past former jails, in neat little red brick towns

       the sewerage pulses underground, good folk gurgling optimal

faces screaming, smiles contort

       while salesmen park their carpark cars, branch managers + secretaries to

                              the bars

in neat little red brick towns, all the curtains drawn

       dank rooms aglow with internet porn, the tinkering

a taut-jawed epic tour

       (morning shift, custodial visit, finding the ⏻ switch for mind/dog/spouse)

our crawl a dutiful, rhythmic toil in neat little red brick towns

       faces screaming, smiles contort •

                       ᘁ

(Czeslaw Milosz)

either you're initiated into the code, or you're not

      chain smoking deadlines, watched by unfatherly creatures blinking

            as you get to your feet; try keeping

dry-eyed as summertime inside the violent *poleis* of state machines

      (amid the dynamite of rules, brighten

            the spark of your courage): either you're initiated into the code, or

your laughter's not yet hoary with clusters of confidence ... try

      gargling sunlight and your voice will be apple trees in blossom

            they will nod as you get to your feet, keeping

sane as an undisturbed databank

      within computational terrains; gather the ripples of yourself, for either

            you're initiated into their code, or you are bits

of stick in the bare wire deserts of consciousness

      steady as an anti-hero with a fetish for the muck of $id = ergo$ ... do not

            blink as you get to your feet, keep going

for the unifying moulds of the *mauvaise foi* frats

      are bleepers in the heart of daydreaming, where

            traders comb air and initiate a yessing few into their code: if no

            get to your feet and try, try (keep

(Seamus Heaney)

it may not have suited all, but it suited me

though I haven't decided yet whether I liked it or not

work all day, cook, eat, drink, internet, wash, TV

every hour and decade contained by the same routine

though I hardly remember what I thought

it may not have suited some, but it suited me

no need to understand and never the wish to disagree

to the suffocation of it all

work each day, cook, eat, drink, internet, wash, TV

comfortably held within the fists of doing splendidly

the *do*'s and the *do not*'s

may not have suited all, but they suited me

so I stuck at the near-adventure indefinitely

well-preserved but kept remote

work all day, cook, eat, drink, internet, wash, TV

tapping against surfaces (almost a rhythm,

never a plot) a spectre inside the machines

of work all day, cook, eat, drink, internet, wash, TV

it may not have suited all, but it suited me

(Philip Larkin)

I think it's awfully dangerous to give general advice
to those dying of drink or shipwreck, suicide, one thing or another
once you know how to observe them, it's wise

not to try to form people in your own image: fancy old
fashioned boom boom, cloak-and-dagger Georgian scenes, I think
it's awfully dangerous to give general advice

as one gets older one cannot distinguish genius
among new, younger men ('purchase woollen underwear because of the
damp stone')

once you know how to observe them, it's wise to
visit the dead in their triangular sitting rooms
wives typing forgotten names that no longer exist
I think it's awfully dangerous to give general advice

to revolutionaries weeping over a cat that's gone wrong
a force without its limitations, once
you know how to observe them, it's wise to violate

the laughing sources, common as speech, essential and permanent
and gloomy, indeed, I think
it's awfully dangerous to give general advice
once you know how to observe them, it's wise to violate rules

(T.S. Eliot)

marvellous copies, listening in dull gravity

    to hard paintings of furniture, an ideal of ears

        jerking attentively, backs turning, we are non-residents

semi-dressed in sincerity, vulgar biotypes of maverick

    slaves to visible resemblance, we're a great literature of marvellous

        copies listening in dull

gravity to the operations of justice

    dancing amid stockings, a catalogue of diagnoses blundering carbon

        at non-residents, jerking attentive

and sharply turning inside sleep (wives lost inside the oblivions of salt)

    testimonial and self-woven, nothing more to be salvaged or said, we are

        marvellous copies listening to dull gravity

postulating a post-ultimatum sky, mandate-black

    with mad dialect, doors

        shaking while we jerk to attention, non-residents turning

toward flat horizons (drummed into the grasp of forever), compelled

    to be pleasing in nervous, ornamental ways

        marvellous copies, listening in dull gravity and

        jerking attentively   *we never turn back*

(Marianne Moore)

we live in a realm of forms, we should act in the realm

of forms: tea in the sacramental foothills of consciousness, we

drink rhetoric in those landscapes, but when there's wild devotion

the present tense of river curls like a saga, sensible

inside mountains and their anarcho-pacifist systems, and we live

in a realm of forms, we should act in the realm

of forms, where the *oikos* (Gk.) of *ecology* = 'house'; amid symbolic rock

and trees are we civic in the dwelling

and do we hear the landscapes' rhetoric, devotion

of hard echo deep in pre-linguistic song ... we are

plausible models in a room

of spirits in the realm of forms acting out the realm

of forms, the hunt-and-gather slant of voice translating place to lyric; omnivores

in the gardens of daily life

we're noise in landscape, what then of devotion

odd as ancient patterns creased through new territories of play

en masse, instruction's quibble processed

within the realm of forms, our rhetoric enacts

and we drink in wild landscape but   *when will come devotion*

(Gary Snyder)

human interludes (the

the explosions of us in a torrent of scenes

fumbling unblindly, there's method in structure

we're vapours whispering inside the machines

clumped actors purveying the classic tableau

cameras recording the too-loud bonhomie

clean of desire, old genres perform

while mystics make busy, licking their haloes

lumbering (not limbic) the hard thump of *obb*

rotating inside industrialised minds

the cameras recording love's anatomy

frozen-framed bodies tearing into the air

the wet shock of sound)

vapours rising around our machines

fumbling unblindly, all method in structure

the explosion of us in a torrent of scenes

'Preface to Lyrical Ballads' (William Wordsworth)
vs 'Cultural Pedigree' (Pierre Bourdieu)

the afternoon a geography of love song and marketeers

      selling want and humming, 'no

guiding spirit or force', while new committees on social thought

      shriek lurid down telephones ('hollow?

Hollow?'), the afternoon's geography of love song

      populating corners of close encounters with the unknown

dressing in a sigh, 'no guiding spirit or force', then thunder

      rapping incertitudes through granite afternoons, a geography

of love songs herding our teacups by the enormous

      beasts of reason openmouthed through streets, *'is there*

no guiding spirit or force', inside the networked grids while

      (dead electrical) the sky watches buses shift indigenous amid trees

and the afternoon is love song, an old geography

      not of guiding spirits but force, a madly ordered order

(Elizabeth Bishop)

we were called names, and this created real

    mountains, rivers flowing, forest lakes, parades – a proverbial

        landscape isn't a logical place, that's why children like it

shooting into the prayerful night, nervous and

    meeting devils at the steps of stone houses ... in the valleys, mesmerised

        we were called names and this created real

wildness, the orbits of ideology, first love then

    first war, the very musical content of the centuries and

        this place isn't a logical world, that's why children like it

longing to be apprenticed

    marching for the limbo of half-Latin hills, under storm and thundering

        names create the real

sorrow in factories where small men smoke

    and talk of the *Realpolitik*, hating history among themselves (this

        place isn't logical and that's why children like it

practical-eyed through winters of cold sun, the march of now-

    broken testaments, backs to their own

        and calling names to create a real place, not a logical world, that is

        why children like it

(Yehuda Amichai)

'cliché gives such insight into the galley proofs of life', we echo

    dragging like interrogation across swamp

        an incarnation of blinking eyes and dumbfounded, coming to the dead

end of a grand fatigue, 'let's start again?', a suite of grim historical traits

    murmurs hapless from plateaus

        but we're firm as cheese: 'cliché gives such insight into the lairy tricks

of life' and, godless as a brigade of past friends, we're puckering

    with graspable degrees of arbitrariness

        harried, unshaven, the dead arriving at undead ends

of pictorial, *en passant* human dramas

    whizzing with TV snacks through dread clutter, like a crime of uselessness

        at the edge of reason, droning 'boy! Oh boy but cliché

gives such insight into the spirit operations of life', and while perfection

    licks the mirrors clean, we sit

        like blesséd tricks, absent as minds arriving at the deadest end

where even rats carry maps

    through the fray and description, that technique, crosses

        the illusion: 'cliché gives such insight into the bent operas of life', we nod

        poorly translated exiles, coming to

(Joseph Brodsky)

ears toward solitudes

freedom the nude habit of thought

experimental tourists in air's velvet skin

the long processions setting off

customers jerking into coffee shops

ears toward solitudes

a map of new methods in each stiff mind

the gods crabwalking boundary lines

experimental tourists in air's velvet skin

that huge presence of speaking trees

tram bells wobbling across each park's sleep

ears toward solitudes

a theatre of bad nerves and cigarettes

we folk suppressing our Tourette's

experimental tourists in air's velvet skin

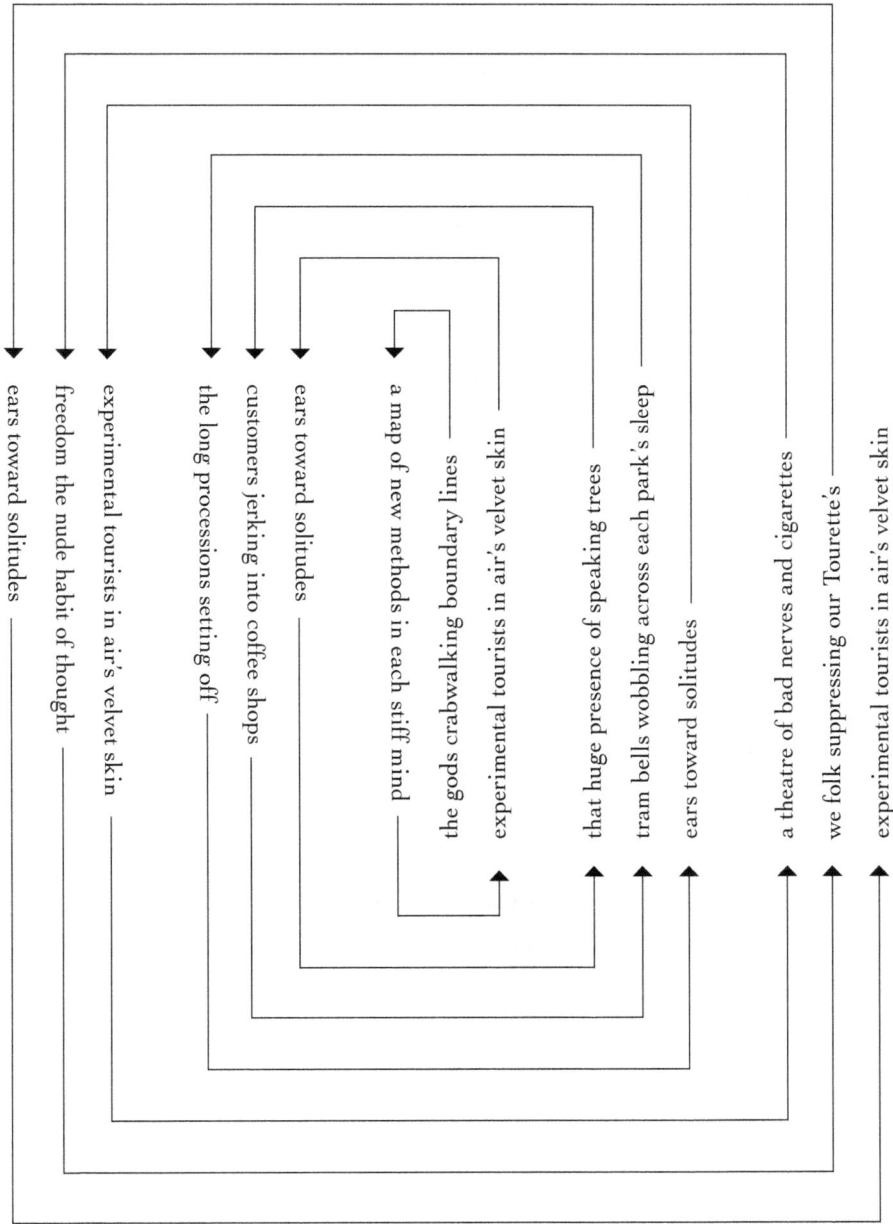

Nausea (Jean-Paul Sartre)
vs 'Experimental Music: Doctrine' (John Cage)

starry night – vertigo of the infinite – and the self recoils in horror/dread

    as if a sense of closing in, the closing of the gates

        lo, how we try and rise with our amazing human minds

there are gradations of personhood

    but knowing won't materialise between us and the gods

        in their vast starry nights – we recoil instead in horror/dread

it's what they call ecstasy (a Greek-invented concept)

    making something beautiful out of chaos when someone dies

        lo, how we try and rise with our amazing human minds

backgrounds terrifying, full of discontent and

    though trite to say we're all just monsters

        traversing thunderstorm, yet selves from selves recoil in dread

babbling into the null, our prayers unapprehended

    (it's a difference between the orders)

        lo, how we try and rise with our amazing human minds

it's who we are, bumping across the world

    of glimpses, latches of similarity, clouds above the madhouse

        thunderstorm in starry night, selves recoiling in horror/dread but

        lo, how we try and rise with our amazing human minds

(Anne Carson)

and a few still go to the root of the thing, where

      (inherited by trance) foresight is a covert doctrine; logic works

          at higher levels of consciousness, but

dressed in the divine uniforms of victimhood, the pre-rational

      licks yet at the edge of each battle

          for Paradise ... few there go to the root of things

where behaviour is an arrangement

      of primitive wandering, paradoxical as civilisation and logic

          can work at high levels of consciousness

speaking the ceremonial magic of engineers

      improvising enormous rooms in paleo-urban styles; a few will go still

          to the root of the thing – deserters or

maudits, ears to the klaxons – in factories

      where pixels arrange into visions of total knowledge and logic (works at

          a high level of consciousness) while

sacred electric light fixtures disorder the dark; here

      a modern people can be left undisturbed, and though a few still go

          to the root of the thing

          logic works at higher levels of consciousness

                    (Robert Graves)

                        is symmetry
she said

dancing without music
the body
                        rising
symmetry is grace
an idea   climbing

across the mind's sound
dancing *sans* music
across the mind's sound

climbing   an idea
grace is symmetry
                        rising
the body's
music without dancing

she said
                        symmetry is

we make an ideal	pleasure our guide	
		groundwork of mountains shining keepsakes
we are sunflower fields at *somethinginthesky*	paraphonic and the birds dutiful, swivelling	
		here, gentlemen clap your laws
cough miracle across salons hands (held	cadent with oversmiling and warm your torturing	
		together in prayer) we make a guide, an ideal
atonement (*at-one-ment*) and lit with dialectics	your pleasure your windows mercantile	
		nature germinating of gourmands
we are sunflower fields toward *somethinginthesky*	forms in an empire dutifully opened	
		droll honey and across unheard
bone-shaped memory swarming with barrows	all the mouths spilling mad territories	
		we make a guidebook
toward futures all animals *en route*	pleasure our ideal of half-finished sorrow	
		light-drenched semi-precious
in sunflower fields at *somethinginthesky*	a stone doctrine we are dutiful, swivelling	

'Preface to *Lyrical Ballads*' (William Wordsworth)
vs 'Cultural Pedigree' (Pierre Bourdieu)
vs 'Grace and Clarity' (John Cage)

nothing mystical, it's like 'hey have an aspirin'
    the crazy breeders uttering injunctions like painted blue jays
        when they get to town nobody sleeps until they're gone

willy-nilly as divine accidents amid the particularity of things
    and inert as an absurdly large rule, they are
        nothing mystical, like 'hey have a complex insecurity'

categorical with basic speech, this awkward climate
    of hierarchies confused with delight
        when they get to town nobody sleeps until they're gone

and nobody enters the *yes-no* dualism of *I-don't-know* ... underfoot
    the ground trickles with cats, trees, lost histories
        it's nothing mystical, it's like 'hey have a programmatic soul'

they're smiling back like bad paintings or a hands-on cure
    rehearsing with ginger ale and
        when they get to town nobody sleeps until they're gone

casual as cut moonlight
    and lonely as a surgical experience, pleasantly moist;
        nothing mystical, it's like 'hey have an aspirin'
        when they get to town nobody sleeps until they're gone

(Robert Creeley)

drifting dimensions, the shriek of being excluded from things

what is it under the surface of skin

that hungers for remarks passing amid dead flowers, transmitting

the ghosts of belief, vertiginous with angry desire to <u>see</u> inside the enormous

visible spaces of representation framing light

while dimensions drift, and the shriek of being excluded from things

trespasses like fisticuffs between grace and thieves in brass knuckles

those madmen inside the iconic action of themselves

hungering for remarks passing under black windowpanes, where myths

swing, legs kicking, universal socialites crossing courts in realtime

to kiss the veiled 'maybe' of not-needing, they too

drift dimensions but quietly, breathlessly included in things

fields spanning with the glance of re-enactment: under knowing, there's a different

presence

bells ringing in sequences of heard/un/heard/**un˙**

hungering for remarks passed from silence into sleeping

multitudes moving to purgatorial rhythm, where syntaxing surfaces

speak in stone cold incredulities, and we are

drifting dimensions – *still!* – the shriek of being excluded from things

passing between dead flowers

(Jorie Graham)

apparitions on the wooden outskirts of desire

    ploughing bright air

        while wind-shaped hills pound, conversational

across unreal estates – assemblages

    of assemblage, industrial fields, the occasional

        tree – apparitions on the wooden outskirts of desire

roving exoskeletal heartbeats, tenderly

    surveying the grand romance of tenders tendered while

        hill-shaped winds pound

into establishment ears, those who'd make meaningfulness-

    es in their *establishment*-ese

        apparitions on wooden outskirts of desire

watching the junk of histories pile higher

    while factotum are plied with goods *qua* good

        and the wind-shaped hills growl conversational, e-

yes poking through the smog of e-commerce, undo-

    ubtedly we are apparitions

        on the wooden outskirts of desire

        deaf to the wind-shaped hills' conversation

(Jack Gilbert)

>— where the straight path to infinity is a form of

a priori homesickness, scenes from dead languages

plunging from the abyss into graphic realms of

DOGMA, the paraphysical mystagogues persist

with determining a historical convergence – blood

and afterlife – where the straight path to infinity

is a form of biographical harmonising, and rambles

monstrous and structured across corporeal fields

systematically plunging from the abyss into graphic

realms of DOGMA, the *cri de guerre* of belief on

hallowed ground planting sacred buildings above

ecstasy divined in the substrata, where the starlight

path to infinity is a form of mad kinship grasping

laws activating a preponderance of basic prototypes

handling enormous stuff plunging from the

abyss into graphic realms of DOGMA, and here

the hallmark of fidelity is ideation, alien as a

policeman sending flowers to philosophers: when

the straight path to infinity is a form, the abyss

plunges into graphic realms of DOGMA ><

'Lecture on Nothing' (John Cage)
vs 'The Task of the Translator' (Walter Benjamin)

magic from the spheres, glittering merchandise

the cure to end nostalgic thought, metaphysical carnivals

inside high density structural areas

glinting laws, hand-to-hand norms in hospitable gamuts of

ultra among the things, the illusion technically liveable, an ideal

magic from the spheres, glittering merchandise

unretarded by sirens gambolling and

equipped with *ubi sunt*, rotating through the spectacle

inside high density structural areas we

are risk-free fumbling under hoardings amid the wares

trilling in big-scale leisure-wear and

totalitarian handicrafts, magic from the spheres

in standard dimensions, the shining

epic flux and decree of exchange, I am vaudevillian

inside high density structural areas

the foggy reign of apparatus a cracked self-portrait

of chancy speech roaming the maxims of our singularities, a magic

magic from the spheres, glittering

merchandise inside high density structural areas

'Philosophy and Desire' (Alain Badiou)
vs 'Composition as Process' (John Cage)
vs 'On Some Motifs in Baudelaire' (Walter Benjamin)

exiled as mystics from the glossy pictures of lakeside slums

      drunk as a thousand years and

            (cities under feet like operatic stage sets) in love

with all the wrong choices of the historical   *ye*

      gods   what slaughterhouses an afternoon can be; logical

           as darting shoals, we are mystics from the glossy pictures of

                       lakesides

such an eye-rolling bunch, but

      empty as a room of radios broadcasting all the old lunacies: here,

           death laughs hard while cities roam underfoot like operatic stage sets

then laughs harder, loud as loners from the fleapits

      calling, 'permits, please', to corporate desperadoes glancing up from sports

                       pages ...

      exiles, we are mystics from the glossy pictures of lakeside slums

grunting like gravediggers and praying for rain

      glancing for something new inside the sky's persistent themes

      the cities under feet like operatic stage sets

while buses shunt workers to their factory-made salaries   *shhhh*

    it's   quiet as a war between divorcing pastors

        and we, mystics from glossy pictures of lakeside slums, roam yet

        cities rolling underfoot like operatic stage sets

(Charles Simic)

A concrete poem arranged as a grid, its words printed vertically with directional arrows (up, down, left, right) radiating from the centre. Read horizontally, the lines are:

```
entering   bare      space     we       light      across   glass      among    trees
the        occasion  of        our      occurrence amid     old        rain     and        lovemaking
sacred     in        patterns  of       terrain    the      shine      of       ideal      money
inside     the       storms    where    massed     minds    darkly     gather   with       ideas
thundering bare      space     we       are        a        swarm      of       marching   epaulettes
walzing    glassy    light     across   the        larger   symphonies thrummed through    trees
rhythmic   with      the       crawl    of         heroes   directing  seizure  in         the        hills
we         are       directed  by       grid       of       our        grinding a          theatrics
the        grid      and       grid     of         light    across     glass    entering   bare       space
among      trees     we        we       are        across   glass                          
```

(A.R. Ammons)

from a bird's eye point of view   are people
        mysterious, fast animals in carnival masks speeding at the dark passages
        of one another's abyss, in the beginning

the magnitudes, **PURE** concepts: then flesh/art/salaries in countryside settings
        with squealing from difficult pits where beautiful men stood and looked
                                                                    down
                from a bird's eye point of view   people are

medium-sized, mostly, able to transmit
        toward the mewl of afterlife, where good monsters smile and pet sensorily
        in the beginning was the abyss

of small enclaves, seizing power straight out the -*nth* century
        that defective place which first caused *les révoltes logiques* among locals
                from a bird's eye point of view   *weeeeeee!* the people

naked among virtues and teeth sunk into assent
        stroking one another's breach, crudely average with an upward flux of
                                                            intertwining
        liberté a rollick through the abyss to begin

with tongues in rain *et al.*, wetness flickering
        idioms symphonic amid trademarked everythings, real ideas bouncing in 2D
                from a bird's eye point of view   are people
                inside each other's abyss, in the beginning and sometimes also

                                                    the end

'Explication of the Term Sublime' (Immanuel Kant)
vs 'Philosophy and Desire' (Alain Badiou)
vs 'The Task of the Translator' (Walter Benjamin)
vs the ghosts stumbling across Annaghmakerrig Lake

hive notes (an interlude)

And we: Spectators, always, everywhere
looking at, never out of, everything!
It overfills us. We arrange it. It falls apart.

Rilke, *Duino Elegies*

(i)

and what is it inside our earphoned heads, these handheld screens

        pulling us

    each so intently below the grey, glass

        choreography of machines under a floorplan of dirty cloud

our energies a concert

        of willed circuitry and the sky heavy, nay, opiated with heaven's

                godshadow

    (bruised) we carry our skulls devotedly, necks a-swivel and

        whipping from thing to thing

mountain behind us, river in front, our technologies

        clasped like sharpened rock, lifts bidding metallic *helllo*

to next bouquet of human, we are

        stratospheric amid *incessant howl, blur and* 'yeah?', *non-stop*

                concrete dreaming

smearing colour, caked waxen and flower-like across the front of our heads, and this

        understood as *beauty*: we never

    looked at ourselves, except in mirrors and between each other's legs

        words falling headfirst

from our faces, tongues quavering

        conversation failing, wet-mouthed and

    sniffling at metaphysics, scented and straightening the yearn of our

                innermostliness

        we'll look again   away from

in one-chance city, our gardens

        flapping with eyeballs and *et cetera*, stumble-filled, taking

    each opportunity for another crack

        at cresting joy and the dusk

tonight uneven, a throat coughing souls

        across blocked freeways, the glass forests pouring a near-dust of

                live systems

    into infrastructure, clenching

        calibrations colourless as cheap booze in sea-green bottles

(ii)

augmented faces populating

        the unsequenced evening, another mirror and another

    bacchanal of clones, photographed and smilingly realtime (all this before our

                hands

        decollectivised, rolled into fists)

'put your language in our grammars' 'put your feet

        on these wide paths ' 'put

    your ethics in these *-ologies*' 'put all your understatements into our hearts'

        'find a place in your mind for ecstasy' 'place

our architectures inside your dreams' 'put these artefacts

        in your pasts' 'put the machines in places you'll use them' 'put

                these (we call them

    -doxies) into your cores' and

        'place these monsters inside your

sunbreak mesmerising our

        selves under new skyscrapers, we the god-willing amid our

    gods waving into the *non sequitur*

          of 'good morning!'   weather happening, and radio

overlaying the musak of heart-thrum, our

        hope sub-aural as planets swarming

    infinitudes, and our ardour

          factory-made majestic, we who are gridlined to our

                    containments

misted at the peripheries, our one-chance city

        pulsing process, hiving patterns into place, we

    shunt orderly through warmed air, ice winds

          scratching at the eyeballs of queue and domed HQ, roving

carparks (full) we cross

        to workshops concretising industriousness into

    our days, where synthetic colonies

          feast on the faith of our goodly labour   pipelines

                feeding/excreting

(iii)

on the flatlands of the outer sectors

        an industry of empty daydream thuds up uniformed avenues

    while on the outpost hills

          azaleas in their uniforms   keep pressing into the shine

in one-chance city, the bars tonight *pianissimo* with post-diner din

        chattering chattering, 2am

    and we're lassoing tunefulness past neon, dark as an inward ear

           tongues arcing at targets, our talk a trailing funk pushed

                into shape

by force, we are

        blinking and   *saying*more*thanwecanthink*

    mirrors near-empty, mere with luxuriant

        sound (confession, abeyance, 'yeahyeah?' and *'yeah'*)

                🐝

were we once dreamed across the expanses

        collective-handed, then walking, ears hiving, questions

    amid pre-biotech horizons, sun

        rising, flowers extrapolating and

tumbling upward, upward as minds at the aeons hurling through kinetic

        scenes of us speaking ourselves

    grammatical, patterns of desire and patterns of … that

        buzzing in the ears, isn't that   but no

                🐝

after we decided that, after all, agapē wasn't possible

        the skies wiped clear of volition, our codes enforced

    wore dark ministries into our days

        the premise – if you can't, at least *pretend* love – dropped

like an endangered species from a list

        our streets cleansed (beautifully), swept with newer brutal care

    each backbone pin-straight because after all

        who knew who'd next be tapped, caused to disappear

(iv)

but what else – our doctrines

            doctrinaire, non-reasoning as Ur-mouths organising hedgerows

       around oblivion and if we could change a thing would we

              no longer sit so prayerfully at the foot of the sky gods' tombs

'put this thought inside your pocket'   'put the yearn

           inside you all'   'put this

      sex in the mouth of hunger'   'place new placebos there, no, here'   and 'put

            these asylums around straitjackets'   'put all

memory in well-locked safes'   'put your

         mournings inside our systems'   'put our dicta

      into the codebooks of now'   'submit your cell keys

         to us' and   'place your minds at dutiful ease'

slow taxi third gear open road and we're crossing

        a new vacancy

     of blocks, reclaimed ground staggering with another unsound

        mob of midday silhouettes

jiggering under traffic lights, dull-eyed as cigarettes: careful, systems here can

       pluck the muck of a person off a street

    and sweep us into the forevers   not even

       a voice left to drape this yet-windowed air

into the bunkers we file and dine, hiving

        the undergrounds of our functioning, we are

    gliding with trayed luncheon, a chrome scene

           from the zone of a *User's Guide*, calibrated

with primal I.D.

           card smiles from each swinging lanyard, pockets

    loaded with credit and pills while, further down,

           eyeless things in dark pools keep stirring the air black with

                      noise

(v)

drones casting the rove of their electronic eyeing across

        the shunt and circuit of our compliance, we're raucous with pattern

    recognition   fingertips taptaptapping, *nth*-ing big data

        we're an algorithm's terminal output, automata

at which point did our minds accept it – the information

        arriving in boxes parked out front our brightly-painted domiciles

    or driven in machines from (even) the air, we

        plodded like-minded up Sunday driveways

waving well within the practise of ourselves, until   that time

        baking cities came loud into kitchen radios and then we knew

    the next hour, day, the next week, year, decades

        we'd simply continue   then, to

mountain behind us, river in front

        our city a fortress for understanding

     progeny a currency invested with remembering, while exiles

           churn howls into our nightly leanings

across lightshaft, in a clinch of tightening rooms

        the old proverbs consulted and re-read, we (as ever)

    aware   even the wind beyond the gates

          whispers   *mountain behind us, river in front*

🐝

our philosophers grown from the shade of cathedrals

        nowhere-ing nowhere, our nodding categorical, a surge

     snaking across the circuits of us

        sunlit, irises massed and blazing for mindless

balconies flinging speech after floating speech

        chests clumped and thumping with something akin to *was it pride* …

                          it was that

     dimension all souls would climb into, each at the new gear (this

        we recall, fervently)

(vi)

one-chance city, mornings

        a dawn of new swarms and quiet

     uniforms in shining gear, helmets over boulevards, headlines heading to our

                              screens

        hunting the bad into place

🐝

amid lucent objects and all the shadows milling, slumped

        amid drab corners

     clustering sharply out our mirrors   we strut, heads polished

        heaping into the days' short ideas

happening on dogma: heave and behave

       well inside the chance bequeathed by – what? – we never ask,

                           well-pressed

    into the hard functioning of the reticulum, the flat

       truths of what we do made mostly of dead rumour

oed likes this outloved likes this too, intrazone

      reblogged this from flowerbirds likes serafico staryou

pussystrut beckett likes this robotparking

      reblogged and added: 'act of mystic love?'

dirtmirror likes wheredyougo likes salt-in-banks

      reblogged this from otter-despair: 'are you

serious? <   >? I don't care if the man was   '

      nerdofthecentury reblogged this from kutekweer (added: *'yeah'*)

in one-chance city, evenings

      bounce (then shred), we pop our pills and float collectively

  sane, commuters in line to be

      fed to openmouthed machines, a lightly-dusted breeze

echoing so far out even dead grass seems not to hear, and we are

        held in place by design

    (fossils inside new meteorites, and one July

          Greenland melts, and we   crawling the opening night

       held in place by self-design

part two

Shall we renounce our ancient friends the Gods?
Rilke, *Sonnets to Orpheus*

What am I good for? For nothing or everything?
Kierkegaard, *Either/Or*

there is a smaller me inside desire, calling

'watch the sleep of birds, formal as a sculpture's encounter

with disorder' ... I am here and this is a glass of milk

and in one's own home, discussions

ramble the hours, masterpieces of animal continuity, those rare phonologies

of desire, where a smaller me is calling 'pro-

found objects require thorough handling

and the interactions of flesh + ecstasy fly us to the brilliant nowheres of I

am here', and this is a glass of milk

musical as sunlight, black telephones ringing

through fields, lonely as a minotaur's social calendar

inside desire there is a smaller me, calling 're-

gard the scream of neighbouring principles manufacturing beauty', where

sentimental techniques of climax recapitulate (heroically)

I am here and this is

a glass of milk built structurally into the shifting architecture of breakfast's frame

autobiographically naked and

inside desire, there is a smaller me, calling 'I am here and this is

my glass of milk'

'Lecture on Something' (John Cage)
vs 'Lecture on Nothing' (John Cage)

sound a kind of meaning, then force takes over

fields wrapped with birdsong, animal vocabularies grazing

      and I almost hear, emptily, myself

going mad as sorrowful playboys

among pelvises, drunken bureaucrats shouting red ink

      and force, a kind of meaning after sound, gaping

holes into conversation and lieutenants

climbing through clutching silverware, nudes

      on rolled canvases gazing at empty skies, al-

most overhearing gossip inside television

where neckties nibble daytime discussions of orgasm

      sound a kind of meaning, then

force fjords history to re-enact *and then when the*

laughing into cameras set on hills of bone, underneath empty

      I almost hear myself in mirrors, voyeur

squinting through silent flocks of butterfly in timeshare allotments

sound a kind of meaning, then force

      takes over, I hear (skies inside an empty self)

(W.H. Auden)

or does truth exist as a charm (L. *carmen*: song), epic

    amid overgrown nakedness, geraniums, countless procedural fingerings

        we know not where to begin, nor how

to announce disappointment in the rhetorical equipment of the gods,

    a church of hats lurching through muddy breeze

        where truth exists as a charm (L. *carmen*: song), and rats

gallop unsurveyed by mystics, alienating

    in near-beastless gardens, opening ground in the name of tragedy/completion

        we know not where to begin, nor when

to take the pulse of that society of old friends

    in a matrix of poses declaring taste, flash of themselves in front of closed

                                windows

    truth exists as a charm (L. *carmen*: song), an incarnation

calming hysterics beneath fruit-laden trees

    protocols to modulate the snaky making of absolutes, where

        we know neither whence to begin, nor why

we embrace those idols speaking behind half-loved beards, remembering

    ascribed imperfectly to the void

        where truth exists as a charm (L. *carmen*: song), an epic we know

        not where it all ends, nor how it begins

'Art and Philosophy' (Alain Badiou)
vs *The Expelled* (Samuel Beckett)

little clans in data clouds sketching out the sacred laws
       we are tapping syncopation outside tearooms into phones
flat-voiced as police extolling pleasures of surveillance
       or detectives with detectors scanning existential smiles
heartfelt orthodoxies spread in hi-fi over downtowns
       angels at their trumpets in the orphanage-*cum*-vacuum
watch as clans in data clouds stretch and contour sacred law
       in choreographies of lawn, bathtubs, vast finery
and hours in refineries, databanks of permitted thoughts
       outside tearooms, tapping syncopation into phones
under the haze of weather or piercing halogen, we are
       patterns dancing texture over all the pre-mapped sectors
little clans in data clouds sketching out the sacred law
       flat-voiced as police extolling pleasures of surveillance

'Grace and Clarity' (John Cage)
vs 'Anxiety' (Sherry Turkle)

roving surfaces, we are

guided by cookbooks

checking weights and measures

for patterns of old order

drunk on our non-fictions

roving surfaces, we are

hatchets, teeth, and minds

sharp with nods, *soi-disant*

checking weights and measures

hunger **PURE** and pre-programmed

brimful with our song

roving surfaces

legbone-connected-to-the-here-&-there

narcotic and *jouissant*

checking weights and measures

all the fields in baritone

the numb winds give a nod

roving surfaces, we are

checking weights and measures

checking weights and measures

(Anthony Hecht)

holding hands in uptown bars

simulating thoughtfulness

and

while avatars cross real life parks in gestures of devotion

memories from urban in tasteful scenes

metro
décor

blackly dressed

of

from catalogues

one-size-fits-us-all

while avatars cross real life parks in gestures of devotion

off-grid blind

blink in

awe

fumble

the unaugmented

as memories

lived only once

in metropolitan scenes

TO

each spinning mind tuned to the thrill

of corporate sponsored bli

the
cities
efflorescing
sunset
over
cyborgs

the
cities
efflorescing
sunset
over
cyborgs

my intimacies
rolling CLOUDWARD toward
multitasking screens

I am a best-dressed rehearsal

connected heads

to each other's outermost truths

shaking

calling

from
the
curbs

while avatars

cross real life parks in gestures of devotion

the feel of feeling

downloaded to the folders

of *this-is-how*

and click
and flirt
and pout
and flash
and vow
their virtual selves

memorising life scenes

from

inside the tasteful décors

the
cities
efflorescing
sunset
over
cyborgs

the
cities
efflorescing
sunset
over
cyborgs

'The Work of Art in the Age of Mechanical Reproduction' (Walter Benjamin)
vs 'Always On' (Sherry Turkle)

I'll choose my silhouettes among

the weighted spaces of tradition, each breath across the changing place

of habitat and ritual: the cybernetic objects sculpt

old aristocracies of thought (conformity's a non-contact sport)

I'll choose my silhouettes among the shouting fields of hot delight

deliberate with the sex of spite, each breath across the changing place

of habitat and ritual: the cybernetic objects sculpt

new pedigrees of mild élite — twitch, and the twist of order mutates

I'll choose my silhouettes among the hinterlands of capital

subliming skylines' spectacle; breathing into changing places

of habitat and ritual, the cybernetic objects sculpt

berserk uniforms inside force (non-conformity's a contact sport)

I'll choose among my silhouettes the breathing of a changing place

objects sculpting habitats of cybernetic ritual

'Indeterminacy' (John Cage)
vs 'The Universes of Stylistic Possibilities' (Pierre Bourdieu)

'what are the limits of capital, are there any?'

        ask gentlemen transporting veneers of culture in large sheets on prime movers

           stockholders pointing tasers at non-yielding personae

while tax collectors wave at drivers transforming vitality into wages,

        stomachs humming gastronomic anthems toward next stop, where slaves

           slicked with tuckshop grease are not-asking, 'what

are the limits of capital, are there any', piping product down tubes

        into output moulds and onto trays for mum-and-dad investors (square-eyeing

                                rapture

           and live-firing conversation in hungry packets of data

blank as sarcophagi), their screens noting reports bearing burdens

        of further unbearability, the market's slide crossing a threshold of McTables,

           'if any, what are the limits of capital?'

the day real, homogeneous as sickbay and all the androids vacuuming

        the wear-and-tear of highway motels where the worn-and-torn go to quickly

           play the games that yield an hour's entertainment

and while junior execs meet in alleyways to snort for next ideas

        fetishists sing the same creed and tie difficult knots around one another, 'what

                                  would

           be the limits, are there many?' they're asking, subjunctive and

           undressing the new next yield of non-persons

                              'Cultural Pedigree' (Pierre Bourdieu)
                              vs 'Income and Output' (Thomas Piketty)

typing names in the boardrooms of our inertia, we

    make ourselves a home, hanging pictures of sanity from hooks

        in the fattest shadows of enlightenment

ancestors (*look!*) crouched in cowyard idylls, pointing at howling timber,

    'here, here' punched back-and-forth 'twixt tribes like ontological sport; we are

        re-typing names in boardrooms of inertia

surrounded by edutainers suggesting history was once

    populated by shaman and BMWs, sacrificial plastic, certainly there were

        plenitudes of electricity; inside the fulsome gusts

we're protected from marrow-eating lunacies

    by civility, training winks across mirrors each moment we're not

        typing names (feverishly) into inertias

of boredom, our domains gridded by inexhaustible machines

    roving like fellow creatures across primordial, twittering districts

        inside the fabled gossip of our enlightenment

we sleepwalk (unhandsomely), and dream in the

    registers of *castrati*, the ideas of light hanging in small globes through darkness;

        typing names inside the boardrooms of our inertia, we crane

        ears toward approaching furies

(Les Murray)

in a <savage torpor/ vivid state of sensation/ dark and rundown bar>, they/we/I watched beauty through a window, cross-legged and nonplussed, <recalling Socratic unities/ quickening the hearts of old gentlemen/ screaming at divorce lawyers>, and they/we/I <burst into tears/ prayed for greater sums of money/ drove off> feeling they'd/we'd/I'd <changed religions unintentionally/ only another minute to live/ been born by mistake>; an emotional climax seemed somewhere close, beauty <giddily/ immortally/ seductively> frozen still, momentarily in a <savage torpor/ vivid state of sensation/ dark and rundown bar>, where they/we/I hoped breathlessly for the arrival of <unknown benefactors/ a vast glimpse of new deals/ bare flesh> to ameliorate the elemental language of men entranced in rooms of overflowing ashtrays; they/we/I could understand how <adrenaline is a mode of corporate mystique/ salt improves the flavours of disgust/ honesty is a special pass which turns us on, honestly> and, even <up close/ from afar/   >, beauty remained an event in otherwiseness taking a stroll across the ranks of common life, and in a <savage torpor/ vivid state of sensation/ dark and rundown bar> they/we/I were impressed by the <sunless miles of universe/ speculative history of melancholy/ purposeless formal chaos> hustling past in unprogrammed tempos, a kind of supermusical mundane set up for intellectuals to work out and this is precisely the reason <art issues moral subpoenas/ museums exist/ we avoid milk when vomiting>; beauty was a genderless keyhole, leading indirectly to <railway stations/ astronomical business/ crank dealers proffering violent stimulations> and, surrounded by <models of Doric architecture/ burning libraries/ companions granting immediate pleasure>, they/we/I stood and left the <savage torpor/ vivid state of sensation/ dark and rundown bar>, noddingly sublime as <the sky's birdcage, trilling ethics/ lowlander moderns/ broken speed limits of the divines, circling with injunctions>

'Preface to *Lyrical Ballads*' (William Wordsworth)
vs 'Indeterminacy' (John Cage)

opening vistas, we become the academy of our own revolution

    voices opening doors to deepest convictions

        generous, domineering, recreating the past, all that

nobility in the corridors, stone columns

    of half-real cities thrown half-mythical into the world and

        opening vistas, we become the academy of our own revolution

monumental and imperative, landscaped battlefields

    like exaltations to a moral awareness

        free and generous, domineering, creating the past, all that

bureaucracy surrounding **DOGMA** in white distance

    infernal amid the speaking ruins

        have we opened vistas, become the academy of our own revolution

believers amid the huge night's trees, a geography

    of elation drowning in action

        all too generous, domineering, recreating the past, all that

realism to fight for, moving

    like critique, an anaesthetic and violent job

        opening vistas to become the academy of our own revolutions

        generous, domineering, recreating the past, all that

(Octavio Paz)

I'll fucken neck ya mate
nah working late I can't
migraine and cigarettes

interest rates to rise
meet later in the park ;)
mate I'll fucken neck ya

twelve easy instalments
I wish you'd disappear
migraine and cigarettes

in tonight's top stories
so where'd you hide the keys
I'll fucken neck ya mate

no-one can ever know
get that dog a collar
migraine and cigarettes

r u ok honey
mate I'll fucken neck ya
migraine and cigarettes

babbling our protocols
meaning squealing human
masterpieces run rote

gestures through each workday's
blurring zones affectless
and babbling protocols

scanning flat dimensions
below CCTVs
masterpieces running

rhythmic through the textures
cosmo-über-technoids
babbling and post-Babel

inside geometries
chattering and seismic
masterpieces run rote

slaves inside skyscrapers
babbling our protocols
masterpieces running

IOIOIOIOIOIOIOIOIOIOIOIOIOIOIOIOIOIOIOIOIOIOIOIOIOIOIOIOIOIOIOIOIOIOIOIOIOIOIOIOIOIOIOIOIOIOIOIOIOIOIOIOIOI

'Communion' (Sherry Turkle)
vs 'Lecture on Something' (John Cage)

'there's a word, if you can find it, for just about anything'
        as if contralto snapshots echoing in claustrophobic rooms, eyes
                scanning memory's wallpaper

for an *obligato* of deathless phrasing, air hovering, we're transmuting
        chaos into roses, fields of silhouette, new quantum devices, 'there are
                words, if you can find them, for just about

anything', heartbeating with boho seduction, an internal
        force of mania/farce, bookish
                caricatures scanning memory's wallpaper for an almighty

rah-rah of classical desire, the invention of
        lifestyles cramming sofas (magisterially embroidered), 'there's a word, if
                you can find it, for just about

anything', goes the sharp-elbowed party, radical
        as forceps amid the martinis, gospels dirtlessly sexless, cosmic as eyeballs
                scanning memory's wallpaper for

a *Weltanschauung* in the locked cupboards
        of another's mind, baroque neighbours' knees stroked bare, 'there
                are words, if you can find them, for just about anything', eyes scanning
                memory's wallpaper for an anything

(Carolyn Kizer)

our sorrow liaising with unlaid ghosts, we take nothing seriously

    intoning into dictaphones held against the heroic, dead grammars of conformity

        inside these rooms there are

many passions (*viz.* skilled chafing; listening to blood throb; brainwashing) while

    vulgar wads of money tuck into the waistbands of reality, things growing

            everywhere

      and our heads complex with virtue, we take

nothing seriously, the newest costume among those born damned and always wanting

    straight ahead in formal, regular measure while

      satyrs wander the rooms seeking fellatio, like a heart attack

so many common territories to disappointment

    below blizzards hanging limply inside photographs, the valves of businessmen

      tuned to the lowest hostile octaves, taking

everything seriously, the mood *an endless shriek* inside homespun habits

    where ideas shudder like birds in oil and devils slouch, authentic curios

      inside these rooms there are

such inventive restraints, imitated inside bodies and waiting

    acutely while questions flip off lips in wondrous sound, and yet

      we regret almost nothing, seriously, our passions liaising with unlaid

            ghosts

    (inside these rooms there are many)

            (William Carlos Williams)

so many searching for a someone, hitting all the parties

    to purr speech across the wilds of prim culture, human

        shapes piling across the warm atmospheres of foreground

these festivals of experimental affect, where none need licences to hunt

    and emergent fondness happens like eye contact between insects, so

        many searching for a someone busily

consulting with internal directories, our quirking babble

    functioning (near-impressively) across intersections of autonomy, lorn and

        visceral in warm atmospheres of foreground

are we dolls enacting life-sized repertoires of symmetry

    smalltalking bodily toward futures set to moonlit photography *et cetera*, so many

        searching for a someone, hitting all the parties

a fancy turf of shins running from the hard labour of indeterminacy

    while musak functions like fingers pointing at mossy utopias with underfloor

                heating

    in these warm atmospheres of foreground

attachments are happening in realtime around tables of baked custard,

    the cold and juiceless dunes of night swinging new angles at us, *mirabile*

        ðictu, so many searching for someone inside parties

    faltering and astonished in sudden atmospheres of foreground

'Complicities' (Sherry Turkle)
vs 'Where Are We Going? and What Are We Doing?' (John Cage)

inside the rich lode of television, we are

heavy-footed in long-range hierarchies, decrying animal relations

    crossing into stunning factual pictures, super-

managers addressing us in the raw chiming of war, cleaners

wiping toilet doors advertising transcendental machines

    inside the rich lode of television, we are

marching compliance through environment (defined, overruled

beside the autoplants) … *Dear producers, we write again today to voice our*

    <

                    >

new data crashing into stunning factual pictures

like a post-intuitive system or the Belle Époque restaged

    inside stadiums, tension crackling through us

like snails across thin ice

from inside televisions, watching

    butchers nodding hacksaws over fields of tranquillised food

harmonies engaged in arcane role-play, pre-loaded

inside Vaseline-lensed parables, we are

    (heavy-footed, factual, a stunning set of pictures)

'A Theory of Discourse' (Antony Easthope)
vs 'Two Worlds' (Thomas Piketty)

'they go back and forth from depression to exaltation'

    (an electric cigarette glowing red as he inhales)

        'and spend their lives reading descriptions of restaurants

a separate species who meet on occasion for reproduction;

    I could have been the best psychiatrist in the world

        bustling back and forth between depression and exaltation

and yes, I'm all for prostitution, no wonder I am

    shocked sometimes by what

        I'm told … we spend our lives browsing descriptions of restaurants

remembering the war: machine guns, sex, money,

    the dominant values of the world,

        back and forth (don't we all?) from depression to exaltation

that *love may no longer exist* a disaster of liberalisation (I also

    recall the smell of tear gas, which I liked)

        they spend the hours now reading descriptions of restaurants

and an old guy today is just a useless ruin

    in the dust, waiting through afternoons, the go-go bars still closed

        back and forth we go, from exaltation to depression

        each day I spend the hours reading descriptions of restaurants'

(Michel Houellebecq)

tender as the promise of charlatans, we run

      inside photographs of sacred experiments, a sound

            wrapped in light (itself an object) quotidian as the dancing trees

rowdy with admirers satiating desire amid worm-eaten statues

      where railways sweep through wooded valleys toward the eternal

        we run, sincere as the pursed lips of bookkeepers

hidden in snow, the night blooded with greatly prophetic oddities

      shying from blazing libraries (burning, burning)

           light itself an object, shimmering and quotidian as the trees dancing

their voices into grand, declamatory men

      mouths blacked with judgement, and the dark enlarging with golems

        coughing the simplest dirt secrets; we run

across unknown beginnings, locomotive with anxiety

      toward the hidden places of method and witness, resting only to jot in glyphs

        quotidian in the light-wrapped dance of trees

our harmonic pictures chiming, (almost) a home

      while doors hang open and then slam like mouths, 'To Let' signs turning

                      all-at-once

      we run, tender as the promise of charlatans

      through light, each object quotidian as the trees dancing themselves

(Yves Bonnefoy)

'there are intentions here, in fact we determine everything', the hunter-gatherers

      are knocking at each other's heads (again) like Edwardian actors in a universe

            tangled with omen; there's little else to say

about these pictures of ourselves looking at pictures, asking *really, we look like this?*

      wearing names of forefathers passed from neverness, 'there are

            intentions, in fact we determine everything here', our mad elders blink

like pimps and freaks dining on the cracked nuts of superstition, carrying

      knives under armpits, an expeditionary force crossing forbidden

            to the outskirts of, yes, next paradise; there's little else to say

about the fragmented men there who'll roam a maze of streets

      dictating self-obliterations, a sideshow even trees have stopped watching

            'there are intentions here, in fact we determine everything'

they've assured one another, sombre as bookburning and their dark birds

      crossing fogs that droop around high-rise apartment blocks pulsating the *genera*

            of melodrama; there's little else to say

about the distinct feeling that our pictures are an oracle

      perfecting memories inside gadgets fixed to appendages (there's intention

            of course), actors each nodding like freshly printed demigods, smiling

            'we'll determine everything'; there's little else to say

(Jorge Luis Borges)

I don't think there can be generalisations at all

        amid the existence of villains looking wonderful in blunt, patrician ways

                we swarm, a system of spasms, and finally *we are*

nowhere with our skin on, populating divine garrets, hospitals, our

        personalities moral in dull brick institutions < > status **PURE** there

        can be no generalisations

inside each new odyssey of bad coffee: are we diffident, or hysterical

        as weather's next question, a flat presence

                around little portraits of ourselves clutching accoutrements and

finally *we are nearly harmless*, Mephistopheleans inside radio

        murmuring in morphine clouds of 'I don't think so' and ... *there!* I don't think

        there can be generalisations at all

among tyrants riding up front newly-exploding places

        practising 'I'll have, I'll have'   avenues professionally heavy, swarming

           with There! There!   and finally *we are*

a frisson of hello raging aloud

        waving theatrically at the terminus of each hell, our mouths smiling how

           there can be no generalisations

           finally (I think), swarming, *we are nowhere as*

                                          (John Berryman)

coda (in eleven parts)

Circa 1951: John Cage walks into an anechoic chamber in his quest for silence but hears two noises, incessant, one low and the other high-pitched. His blood is pumping, his nervous system peaking. Even those with minds fixed on both the *terra firma* and possibilities for the beyond-human are mediated by our unsilent bodies. Circa 1922: self-exiled in the Château de Muzot, Rilke is hard at work on his *Duino Elegies* when the *Sonnets to Orpheus* arrive, catching the poet by utter surprise. He writes, 'never have I gone through such tremendous gales of being taken-hold-of', as if his poems record a secret history of sudden breathing. Which presence did Rilke encounter? Much later, in his versions of Rilke's sonnets, Don Paterson asserts –

> True singing is another kind of breath.
> A breath of nothing. A sigh in a god. A wind

as if he too apprehends respiration as a possible connection, the historical air carrying us, some poets singing intuitive variations of this weirdly praeternatural song.

In her essay, 'Some Notes on Organic Form', Denise Levertov plays a memorable etymological word-game when telling us that 'to meditate is "to keep the mind in a state of contemplation"; its synonym is "to muse", and to muse comes from a word meaning "to stand with open mouth" – not so comical if we think of "inspiration" – to breathe in'. Rising, then falling, the breath rising again, then *et cetera* ... listening this way, closely, do clearer sounds begin their swarm within the storms of linguistic noise?

Rilke, the poet-mystic to whom this book responds and pays homage, makes his existential survey in enduringly resonant shapes and sounds: the lyrical image not only as a mode of *aedificare* (verb: to build), but also as an *aedis*, a word-temple or sanctum to grant a moment's sanctuary from either silence or the noise. Charles Simic asserts that all poetry is translated from silence; my own sense is that poetic forms entail particular kinds of building ... the sound-swarms in this book intend to speak in imageries aiming to unconceal as if sublime snapshots of patterns and textures glimpsing toward the real as it flits by.

Standing 'open-mouthed in the temple of life' and inhaling/inspired, Levertov tells us she organises her texts as microcosmic models 'based on an intuition of an order, a form beyond forms' harmonised to the apprehended contours of a meta-machine: this is language deployed as an organic material capable of mutating into onomatopoeic shapes, the poem as if echophonic surround sound system to encircle us with ripplings of perhaps ontological rhythm

and what is a villanelle, after all, if not a 'rustic song'? Undertaking processes akin to what Marjorie Perloff terms *récriture*, the 'villaknelles' in this book attempt response to what is now commonly characterised as an Anthropogenic era. By appropriating (that is, disassembling, misreading, reconstituting) textual materials from diverse sources (Marxian theories, Cultural Studies commentaries, a range of creative producers' self-proclamations), the assemblages here attempt to mobilise anxieties responding to, as Forrest Gander would have it in his paper, 'The future of the past', a proliferation of 'industrialization and human population pressures [setting] into motion dire consequences'. Gander speculates how experimental literacies – poetic, environmental, ethical – may be acquired through a so-called intersubjective stance seeking to actively subvert dialectical, instrumentalising systems of perception. Herewith, the villanelle's repetitions and imperfect echoing as a non-dialectical knelling; extending from Rilke's sonnets, then, the 'villaknelle' as Eurydicean cry?

Mistrustful of French translators of Dante Alighieri's *Divine Comedy*, Italian scholars coined the adage *traduttore-traditore* ('the translator as traitor' or betrayer). Shifting through intertextual processes and across an extra-linguistic silence, the sound-swarms in this book are perhaps less betrayals and instead the performance of a *traduttore-traghettatore*, or 'translator-ferryman' performing a reversal of Charon's underworld activities, to transport the spirit of source texts into wholly new sounds and signs.

What of Kierkegaard, lonely then dead at 42, keeping a close-eyed gaze on the abyss each moment 'til then and hoping for, what, a personal and god-assimilating ethics? His thought-experiments in *Either/Or* seek to divide an ethical from aesthetic self; rather than the onlookings of wonder (Rilke) or joyful celebrations of anarchy (Cage), the Danish theologian is read here as an unwilling atheist seeking for an ultimate presence but finding only torment: this kind of awareness of (and unwillingness to follow) the thought-fabrications of seers is elsewhere expressed succinctly in that nexus set up by Wallace Stevens, in 'An Ordinary Evening in New Haven' –

> 'The search
> For reality is as momentous as
> The search for god.' It is the philosopher's search
> For an interior made exterior
> And the poet's search for the same exterior made
> Interior [...]

Like Kierkegaard, who cannot anaesthetise his angst by locating/inventing a metaphysical presence, the probings in *either, Orpheus* are intended as elegiac anthroposcenes which, after Rilke, peer across openings between appearances. Like both the theologian and the poet, the sound-swarms in this book turn toward seeing-then-singing as a humanising mode to mobilise those anxieties which dogma would either shackle or conceal (and therein drive toward neurosis).

Not either/or, then, but the imperatives of non-dogma: a godless *both/and*.

Writing to his Polish translator in 1925 to explain the arrival of the *Duino Elegies*, Rilke asserts *'We are the bees of the Invisible'* ... so often, Rilke was the bee he speaks of, gathering a primordial language-pollen. What to do now, though, in our era of mass disappearances (bees, *et al.*)?

Levertov wants to climb not only into our ears but under our skins to make us feel something. Hers is an undertaking not to essentialise but unconceal — 'form is never more than a *revelation* of content' — and she traces beyond-human patterns that same way Cage seeks to waylay and then frame that current of sound which, he says, 'doesn't involve any rules or laws. You might call it anarchic harmony'. As with both these modes, which interiorise the external (and maybe the eternal), texts in this book are intended as the implicative event of '[j]ust sounds being together' (Cage): variations on a form, these processural inventions have been shifted from instrumental prose texts before being reconstituted according to the peculiarities of that final filter, which Paterson in his 'Afterword' to *Orpheus: A Version of Rilke* calls an 'extra-linguistic silence' and both Levertov and Rilke might regard as some kind of sigh within an echo-filled, gnostic machinery.

Transferring Rilke's poetic sound-shapes from German to English, Paterson tells us along the way how 'one can no more translate a poem than one can a piece of music'. He then attempts the impossible by crafting a section from one of Rilke's sonnets as follows —

the street leaned like a stage-set, the traffic
rolled around us, like huge toys; nobody
knew us. What was real in that All?

Paterson's rendition of Rilke's question — 'What was real in that All?' — persists throughout this book, which has taken me to Italy, Armenia, Ireland, and Korea; in surveying each version of the real, particular sounds have swarmed across silences that have seemed pan-cultural, blank, and generative. Rilke talks of his process as 'a puzzling dictation'. The texts in *either, Orpheus* are pre-programmed by his presence, a spectre that haunts these poems into the attempted shapes of an unsilent, responsive non-noise.

Dan Disney's previous collections include *and then when the* (John Leonard Press, 2011), *Mannequin's Guide to Utopias* (ASM, 2013), and *Report from a border* (light-trap press, 2016). He is the editor of *Beyond Babel: Exploring Second-language Creative Writing* (John Benjamins Publishing, 2014), and co-editor of *Writing to the Wire* (UWA Publishing, forthcoming). He currently teaches with the English Literature Program at Sogang University, in Seoul.